HorrorScapes

Ghostly Alcatraz Island

by Stephen Person

Consultant: Troy Taylor
President of the American Ghost Society
Author of *Dead Men Do Tell Tales:*
History & Hauntings of American Crime & Mystery

Credits

Cover and title page illustration by Dawn Beard Creative and Kim Jones; 4, William Silver/Shutterstock; 5, Kim Jones; 6, Kim Jones; 7, © Courtesy National Park Service, Museum Management Program and Golden Gate National Recreation Area, goga3264/www.cr.nps.gov/museum; 8L, © Gerald French/Corbis; 8R, © Ohlone peoples built canoes of tule reeds harvested from the bay marshes and creeksides, Ludvik [Louis] Choris (1795–1828),Drawing, Image courtesy of California Historical Society, FN-30512; 10, © Courtesy National Park Service, Museum Management Program and Golden Gate National Recreation Area, goga2316i/www.cr.nps.gov/museum; 11T, © Courtesy National Park Service, Museum Management Program and Golden Gate National Recreation Area, goga55/www.cr.nps.gov/museum; 11B, Bettmann/Corbis; 12L, © Courtesy National Park Service, Museum Management Program and Golden Gate National Recreation Area, goga40046-008/Darlyne Sheppard Alcatraz Photo Collection/www.cr.nps.gov/museum; 12R, © Associated Press/AP Images; 13, © Courtesy National Park Service, Museum Management Program and Golden Gate National Recreation Area, goga40046-047/www.cr.nps.gov/museum; 14, © Interfoto/Alamy; 15, © Robert Hollingworth/Alamy; 16, © American Stock/Getty Images; 17L, © Corrie McCluskey/Workbook Stock/Getty Images; 17TR, © Everett Collection, Inc.; 17TL, © Harold Hecht/Ronald Grant/Mary Evans/Everett Collection, Inc.; 18, © Charles E. Steinheimer/Time & Life Pictures/Getty Images; 19, © Courtesy National Park Service, Museum Management Program and Golden Gate National Recreation Area, goga18261i/www.cr.nps.gov/museum; 20L, © Albo/Shutterstock; 20R, © Courtesy National Park Service, Museum Management Program and Golden Gate National Recreation Area, goga405/www.cr.nps.gov/museum; 21L, Courtesy of Ocean View Publishing/www.alcatrazhistory.com; 21R, © Everett Collection, Inc.; 22, © Curved Light USA/Alamy; 23, © Ben Peoples; 24L, © Sean Clarkson/Alamy; 24R, © Robyn Beck/AFP/Newscom; 25L, © Pacific Stock/SuperStock; 25R, © Gistimages/Alamy; 26, Courtesy of Richard Senate; 26–27, © Jason O. Watson/Alamy; 28, © Courtesy National Park Service, Museum Management Program and Golden Gate National Recreation Area, goga2316L/www.cr.nps.gov/museum; 29, © Aric Crabb/Bay Area News Group/Zuma Press/Newscom; 31, © dauf/Shutterstock; 32, © 7382489561/Shutterstock.

Publisher: Kenn Goin
Editorial Director: Adam Siegel
Creative Director: Spencer Brinker
Design: Dawn Beard Creative and Kim Jones
Illustrations: Kim Jones
Photo Researcher: Picture Perfect Professionals, LLC

Library of Congress Cataloging-in-Publication Data

Person, Stephen.
  Ghostly Alcatraz Island / by Stephen Person ; consultant, Troy Taylor.
     p. cm. — (HorrorScapes)
  Includes bibliographical references and index
  ISBN-13: 978-1-936087-97-6 (library binding)
  ISBN-10: 1-936087-97-9 (library binding)
 1. United States Penitentiary, Alcatraz Island, California—History—Juvenile literature. 2. Prisons—California—Alcatraz Island—History—Juvenile literature. 3. Ghosts—California—Alcatraz Island—History—Juvenile literature. 4. Alcatraz Island (Calif.)—History—Juvenile literature. I. Taylor, Troy. II. Title.
  HV9474.A53P47 2011
  133.1'2979461—dc22

                                      2010011128

For more information, write to Bearport Publishing Company, Inc., 101 Fifth Avenue, Suite 6R, New York, New York 10003. Printed in the United States of America in North Mankato, Minnesota.

062010
042110CGC

10 9 8 7 6 5 4 3 2 1

Contents

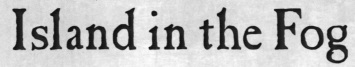

Island in the Fog

Waves crashed against the cliffs of Alcatraz Island. Thick **fog** drifted across the rocky hills. High above the sea sat the most feared prison in the United States. The year was 1945. The time was 9:30 at night—lights-out time at Alcatraz **Federal Penitentiary**.

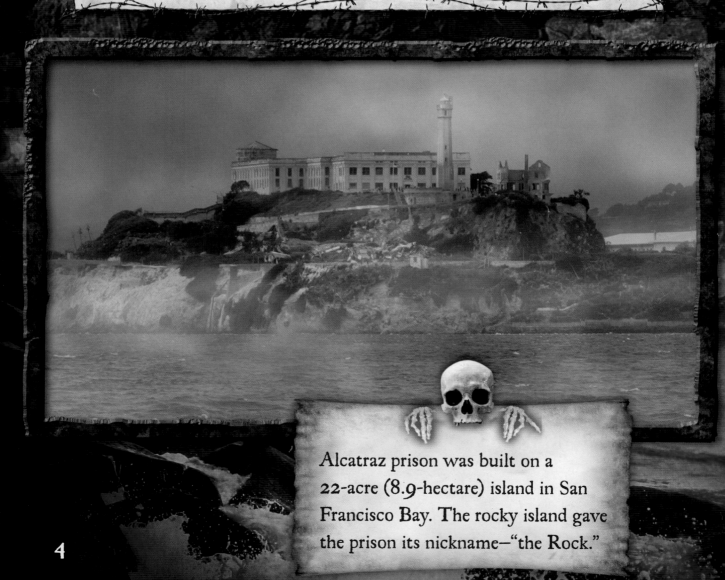

Alcatraz prison was built on a 22-acre (8.9-hectare) island in San Francisco Bay. The rocky island gave the prison its nickname—"the Rock."

Just moments after the prison **cells** went dark, the prisoner in cell 14D began screaming. Someone was in his cell, he shouted. The figure had "glowing red eyes," and was trying to kill him! The guards ignored the shouting. The prisoner was locked behind a solid steel door, and no one could possibly get in or out. The screaming grew louder and louder. Then it suddenly stopped. The guards heard only the normal night noises of whistling wind and crashing waves.

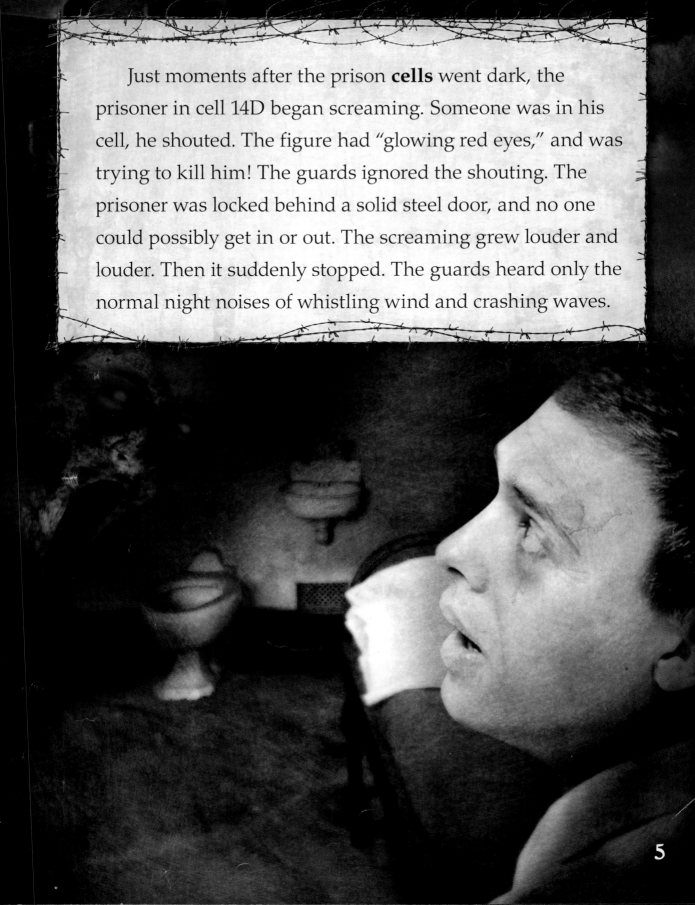

Murder on the Rock

The next morning, the guards slid open the door of cell 14D. The prisoner's lifeless body lay on the cold floor. His neck was marked with dark purple bruises. When doctors did an **autopsy**, they found that the man had been **strangled**. Impossible, said the guards—no one had entered the cell on the night of his death. Doctors refused to believe this. There was no way the prisoner could have caused the injuries to himself.

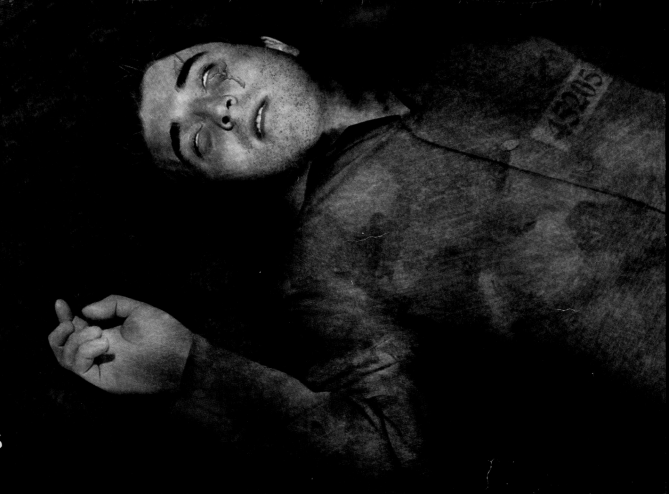

According to one version of the story, things got even creepier. The next day, guards lined up the prisoners. They did this every morning to make sure no one had escaped. There, at the end of the line, stood the dead man! Seconds after the prisoners and guards turned to look, the figure vanished.

Was the tale of the prisoner's mysterious death really true? No, but it is one of the many chilling stories—some true, some not—that people tell about this spooky island.

Alcatraz guards were used to hearing stories about strange creatures haunting the prison. **Inmates** often spoke of seeing the ghost of a man dressed in clothing from the 1800s. Most guards didn't believe the tales.

Guards on Alcatraz Island

The Perfect Place for a Prison

Before becoming a prison, Alcatraz was an island no one wanted. For hundreds of years, the Miwok (MEE-wok) Indians collected birds' eggs there. They never stayed for long, though. According to **legend**, the place was haunted by evil **spirits**. Then in the 1850s, the U.S. Army began building a **fort** on Alcatraz. The fort was in a perfect location to stop enemy ships from entering San Francisco Bay.

Alcatraz Island is surrounded by swirling currents, cold, choppy seas, and winds whipping off the Pacific Ocean.

Native Americans were the first to use Alcatraz as a prison. They punished tribe members by leaving them alone on the island.

Army leaders realized the **remote** island was also perfect for something else—a **military** prison. On a cold day in December 1859, the first prisoners arrived—11 soldiers guilty of violent crimes. The men were tossed in a room called the **dungeon**. This was a dark **chamber** under the fort. The prisoners were given no blankets, and slept on the concrete floor.

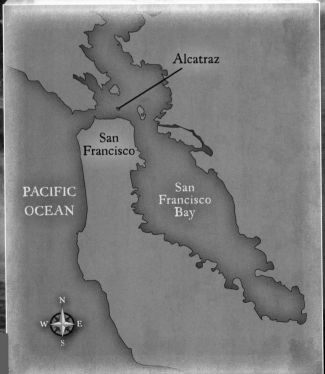

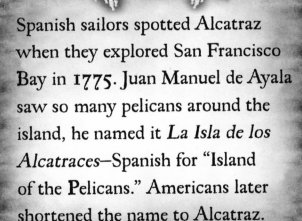

Spanish sailors spotted Alcatraz when they explored San Francisco Bay in 1775. Juan Manuel de Ayala saw so many pelicans around the island, he named it *La Isla de los Alcatraces*–Spanish for "Island of the Pelicans." Americans later shortened the name to Alcatraz.

Alcatraz Island lies 1.5 miles (2.4 km) off the coast of California. Prisoners could see San Francisco, and when the wind blew in just the right way, they could even hear sounds from the city. They found it torture to be so close to freedom—and yet so far away.

9

Escape-proof Island

The army used Alcatraz as a prison for more than 70 years. Only soldiers who committed crimes were kept there. That was about to change, however.

In the 1920s and early 1930s, violent crime was on the rise in American cities. Government leaders needed a place to send the country's most brutal killers. They wanted a prison so secure, no one could escape. They also wanted a prison that would terrify even the toughest **gangsters**. Alcatraz Island was the perfect spot.

In the 1860s, prisoners were woken up at 5:00 in the morning and put to work breaking rocks. Prisoners who broke the rules could be whipped.

Workers added new locks and thicker steel bars to the prison cells on Alcatraz. They also built guard towers. From these towers, guards could watch the prisoners and make sure no one tried to escape. By August 1934, Alcatraz was ready to welcome the country's most dangerous criminals.

Guards in the towers carried Thompson submachine guns. These guns could fire more than ten bullets per second.

Alcatraz was built to hold up to 300 prisoners at a time. There was one guard for every three prisoners at Alcatraz. Other prisons in the United States averaged one guard for every twelve prisoners.

Life on the Rock

Life for prisoners on Alcatraz was not meant to be fun. Guards woke them up at 6:30 in the morning. The men had 20 minutes to eat breakfast. Then they were put to work. **Warden** James Johnston enforced a silence policy. Prisoners were not allowed to talk to one another in their cells. The only times they could speak were when they were sitting in the dining room, working at a job, or attending a group event such as a prayer service.

Prisoners did many jobs at Alcatraz, including serving food in the cafeteria. Most prisoners actually wanted to work—it was better than sitting alone in their cells all day.

James Johnston had been the warden at some of the nation's toughest prisons before taking over at Alcatraz in 1934. He served as warden of Alcatraz until 1948.

After years of prisoners' complaints, Warden Johnston relaxed his silence policy in the late 1930s.

Life was even **harsher** for prisoners who broke the rules. They were tossed into the Hole—a part of the prison made up of five **solitary confinement cells**. Prisoners could be forced to spend up to 19 days by themselves in one of these dark cells. The most feared cell in Alcatraz, however, was the Strip Cell. Prisoners were thrown into this cell without clothes. There was no light, no sink, and no bed. Instead of a toilet, there was a small hole in the cell floor.

Prisoners who behaved well were allowed time outside to talk or play sports.

Alcatraz vs. Al Capone

One of the prisoners brought to Alcatraz in 1934 was the famous gangster Al Capone. By the time of his arrest in 1932, Capone had built a criminal empire worth more than $60 million. All his money couldn't help him at Alcatraz, however. When he tried to **bribe** the guards, they tossed him in the Hole.

From 1920 to 1933, it was illegal to make or sell alcoholic drinks in the United States. Capone made a fortune by bootlegging— or illegally selling alcohol. He became so famous, he was featured on the cover of *Time* magazine in 1930.

Capone spent four and a half miserable years at Alcatraz. One day he got in a fight with another prisoner. The man stabbed Capone with a pair of scissors. After that, Capone was usually seen crouching in the corner of his cell, strumming a banjo. He often refused to come out, even for meals. "It looks like Alcatraz has got me licked," a terrified Capone told Warden Johnston.

The cells in Alcatraz had a sink, toilet, and cot. They were five by nine feet (1.5 by 2.7 m) wide. Prisoners could reach out their arms and touch both sides of the cell at the same time.

Al Capone died in 1947, but some people are convinced his ghost lives on at Alcatraz. Today, visitors sometimes report hearing the faint sounds of banjo music coming from Capone's old prison cell.

15

The Birdman of Alcatraz

Another famous Alcatraz inmate was Robert Stroud. Arrested for murder in 1911, Stroud was sent to prison in Kansas. Behind bars, he developed a love of birds. He studied canaries, raising more than 300 of them in his cell. Stroud was kind to birds—but cruel to people. He stabbed several inmates and murdered a prison guard. In 1942, Stroud was sent to Alcatraz.

Criminals were never sent directly to Alcatraz after being sentenced to jail. Alcatraz was a place for prisoners like Robert Stroud who had committed crimes in other prisons.

Robert Stroud

Alcatraz guards refused to let Stroud keep birds. Considered a danger to others, Stroud wasn't even allowed to be near other prisoners. A movie called *The Birdman of Alcatraz* showed Stroud as a gentle man who was sorry for his crimes. People who knew him told a different story. "That guy was not a sweetheart," said a fellow prisoner at Alcatraz. "He was a **vicious** killer."

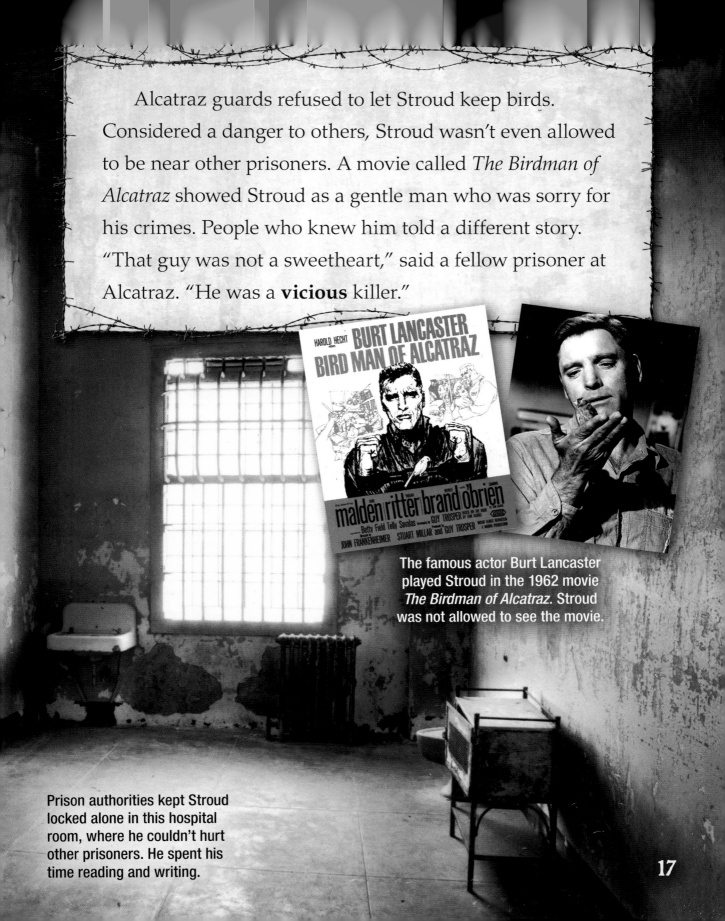

The famous actor Burt Lancaster played Stroud in the 1962 movie *The Birdman of Alcatraz*. Stroud was not allowed to see the movie.

Prison authorities kept Stroud locked alone in this hospital room, where he couldn't hurt other prisoners. He spent his time reading and writing.

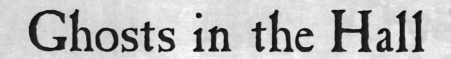

Ghosts in the Hall

Alcatraz was built to be escape-proof. That didn't stop prisoners from trying to break out, though. On May 2, 1946, six inmates broke free from guards. They grabbed guns from a storage room and took control of **Cell Block** C. Alcatraz guards called in the **Marines**. What followed was a bloody, two-day shootout that became known as the Battle of Alcatraz. By the time the Marines retook the building, three of the prisoners lay dead.

Reporters on a boat watching the Battle of Alcatraz

Some say the spirits of the three prisoners never left. Thirty years later, a night watchman walked past the hall where the prisoners were killed. He heard chilling cries and moans. He shined his flashlight down the hall. It was empty. Terrified, the watchman hurried away. In the years since, many visitors have reported hearing the ghosts of the dead prisoners coming from the hall.

Sam Shockley (center) and Miran Thompson (right) were executed for their role in the Battle of Alcatraz. Clarence Carnes (left) was spared the death penalty because he had refused to kill several guards during the battle.

In 14 separate attempts, a total of 36 men tried to escape from Alcatraz. Twenty-three were caught and brought back, six were shot to death, and two drowned. Five are listed as "missing, and **presumed** drowned."

Escape from Alcatraz?

Did anyone ever succeed in escaping from Alcatraz? That's another mystery about this spooky island. On the night of June 11, 1962, three men squeezed into tiny air **vents** in their cells. They crawled through the vents to the roof. Then they climbed down pipes attached to the outside of the prison.

Before escaping, the men built models of their own heads, using soap, paint, and hair from the prison barbershop. They placed the models in their beds so guards would think they were sleeping.

The men ran down to the water, carrying a raft and life vests they had sewn from more than 50 prison raincoats. They **inflated** the raft, climbed in, and pushed out into San Francisco Bay. No one knows what happened next. These prisoners are three of the men Alcatraz lists as "presumed drowned." Their bodies were never found, though, so it's possible they got away.

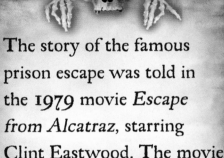

The story of the famous prison escape was told in the 1979 movie *Escape from Alcatraz*, starring Clint Eastwood. The movie was filmed at Alcatraz.

The men spent months chipping away the cement that held the air vents in their cells. These vents let fresh air into the prison.

CLINT EASTWOOD
ESCAPE FROM ALCATRAZ

A Haunted Island?

During its time as a federal prison, 8 men were murdered by other prisoners on Alcatraz, and 5 killed themselves. Another 15 died from illness. When a place sees as much misery and death as Alcatraz, can it become haunted? Warden Johnston did not believe in ghosts. He admitted, however, that some things happened at Alcatraz that he simply could not explain.

The warden's house lies in ruins today, which only adds to its spooky feel.

One Christmas, some people say a ghostly figure appeared at a party in the warden's house. The room suddenly turned cold. The fire in the stove went out. A moment later, the figure vanished.

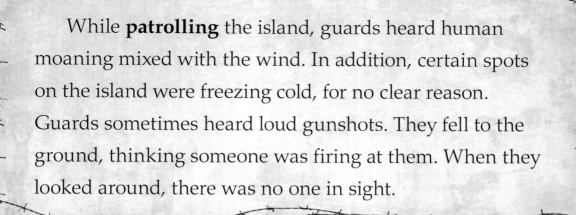

While **patrolling** the island, guards heard human moaning mixed with the wind. In addition, certain spots on the island were freezing cold, for no clear reason. Guards sometimes heard loud gunshots. They fell to the ground, thinking someone was firing at them. When they looked around, there was no one in sight.

On some nights, people swear they can see the old Alcatraz lighthouse, its light flashing in the fog. This is not so amazing, except for one thing—that building was torn down in 1909. It was replaced with the lighthouse, shown here, that still stands on Alcatraz.

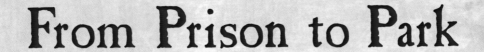

From Prison to Park

Alcatraz was a perfect place for a prison because it was hard for inmates to get off the island. Unfortunately, however, it was also hard to get things to the island. Everything had to come by boat, including fuel, food, and drinking water. Alcatraz cost the government about $10 a day per prisoner in 1959—compared with $3 at other prisons. To save money, officials shut Alcatraz down on March 21, 1963. Inmates were moved to other prisons around the country.

Today, more than a million curious people visit Alcatraz every year.

A total of 1,545 prisoners were he in Alcatraz between 1934 and 19 The average stay was eight years.

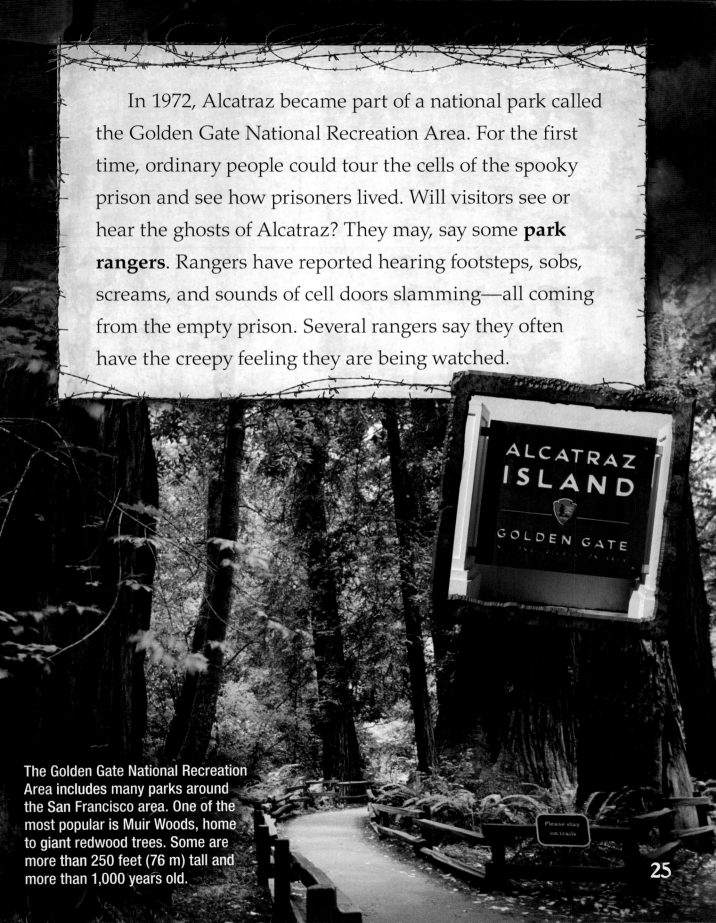

In 1972, Alcatraz became part of a national park called the Golden Gate National Recreation Area. For the first time, ordinary people could tour the cells of the spooky prison and see how prisoners lived. Will visitors see or hear the ghosts of Alcatraz? They may, say some **park rangers**. Rangers have reported hearing footsteps, sobs, screams, and sounds of cell doors slamming—all coming from the empty prison. Several rangers say they often have the creepy feeling they are being watched.

The Golden Gate National Recreation Area includes many parks around the San Francisco area. One of the most popular is Muir Woods, home to giant redwood trees. Some are more than 250 feet (76 m) tall and more than 1,000 years old.

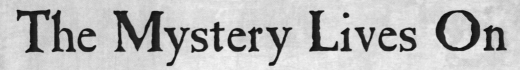

The Mystery Lives On

Some people come to Alcatraz hoping to find ghosts. Richard Senate is one of those people. He is a ghost hunter who travels the world looking for evidence of ghosts. One foggy evening, he took his search to Alcatraz Island. Senate was going to spend the night in America's most haunted prison.

Richard Senate has investigated more than 250 haunted sites around the world. "Alcatraz Island was confirmed as a true haunted site," he said after his visit.

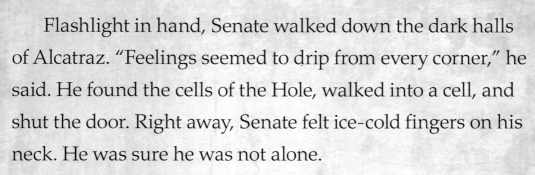

Flashlight in hand, Senate walked down the dark halls of Alcatraz. "Feelings seemed to drip from every corner," he said. He found the cells of the Hole, walked into a cell, and shut the door. Right away, Senate felt ice-cold fingers on his neck. He was sure he was not alone.

Senate was lucky, though. Unlike prisoners in the Hole, he could escape from Alcatraz whenever he wanted. The next morning Senate got on a boat and sailed away from the ghosts of Alcatraz. "It was a night I shall never forget," he said.

Many visitors believe that the Hole is the most haunted place on Alcatraz Island.

Senate shut himself into cell 12D in the Hole. He was hoping to meet a ghost—and was not disappointed.

ALCATRAZ:
Then and Now

Then: Hundreds of years ago, Native Americans believed Alcatraz Island was haunted by evil spirits.

Now: Many believe the island is haunted by the spirits of prisoners who suffered or died at Alcatraz.

Then: The U.S. Army began to build a fort on Alcatraz Island in the 1850s. At that time, San Francisco was a growing town of about 20,000 people.

Now: San Francisco's **population** today is about 800,000, making it one of the largest cities in the United States.

Then: Prison guards and their families lived in apartment buildings on Alcatraz. The children took a 7:30 A.M. ferry to school in San Francisco.

Now: Park rangers and other workers commute by ferry in the opposite direction—from San Francisco to Alcatraz.

The daughters of prison guards stand on an old army cannon at Alcatraz. Children also enjoyed roller-skating on the steep island roads, playing hide-and-seek in the fog, and bowling in a two-lane bowling alley.

Then: From 1934 to 1963, Alcatraz was a maximum-security prison, housing some of the nation's most dangerous criminals.

Now: Alcatraz is a national park, open to visitors from around the world.

Then: The cold water and strong currents of San Francisco Bay helped scare prisoners out of trying to escape. Several people who did try to swim off the island are believed to have drowned.

Now: People make the 1.5-mile (2.4-km) swim between Alcatraz and San Francisco just for fun. Swimmers must be in top shape, and they must train in cold water before making the swim.

Today, some people enjoy the challenge of swimming from Alcatraz to San Francisco.

Glossary

autopsy (AW-top-see) an examination of a dead person that is used to find out the cause and time of death

bribe (BRIBE) to offer money or a gift to get someone to do something that is usually wrong

cell block (SEL BLOK) a section of a prison

cells (SELZ) rooms in a prison in which prisoners are held

chamber (CHAYM-bur) a closed-in space or room

dungeon (DUHN-juhn) a dark prison cell, usually underground

federal penitentiary (FED-ur-uhl *pen*-i-TEN-shuh-ree) a prison run by the national government

fog (FAWG) a thick cloud-like mass of tiny water droplets that floats close to the ground

fort (FORT) a strong building from which people can defend an area

gangsters (GANG-sturz) people who are part of a group of criminals

harsher (HARSH-ur) more difficult; more cruel

inflated (in-FLAY-tuhd) blew up with air

inmates (IN-mayts) prisoners

legend (LEJ-uhnd) a story handed down from long ago that is often based on some facts but cannot be proven true

Marines (muh-REENZ) a branch of the U.S. military; Marines are trained to fight on both land and at sea

military (MIL-uh-*ter*-ee) having to do with soldiers and the armed forces

park rangers (PARK RAYN-jurz) people who look after parks and forests

patrolling (puh-TROHL-ing) protecting an area by walking around it to watch for trouble

population (*pop*-yuh-LAY-shuhn) the total number of people living in a place

presumed (pri-ZOOMD) believed to be true without proof

remote (ri-MOHT) difficult to reach

solitary confinement cells (SOL-uh-*tair*-ee kon-FINE-muhnt SELZ) a section of a prison in which a prisoner is locked away from other prisoners; it is used for special punishment

spirits (SPIHR-its) supernatural creatures, such as ghosts

strangled (STRANG-uhld) choked to death; killed by stopping one's breathing

vents (VENTS) openings that carry air into or out of a building

vicious (VISH-uhss) violent and dangerous

warden (WAR-duhn) a person in charge of a prison

Bibliography

Barter, James. *Alcatraz.* San Diego, CA: Lucent Books (2000).

Esslinger, Michael. *Alcatraz: A Definitive History of the Penitentiary Years.* San Francisco, CA: Ocean View Publishing (2008).

Martini, John Arturo. *Fortress Alcatraz: Guardian of the Golden Gate.* Berkeley, CA: Ten Speed Press (2004).

Wlodarski, Robert J. and Anne N., and Michael J. Kouri. *Haunted Alcatraz: A History of La Isla de los Alcatraces and Guide to Paranormal Activity.* West Hills, CA: Ghost Publishing (1998).

Read More

George, Linda. *Alcatraz.* New York: Children's Press (1998).

Higgins, Christopher. *Alcatraz Island.* Philadelphia: Mason Crest Publishers (2004).

Sloate, Susan. *The Secrets of Alcatraz.* New York: Sterling (2008).

Learn More Online

To learn more about Alcatraz, visit
www.bearportpublishing.com/HorrorScapes

Index

UNITED STATES PENITENTIARY
ALCATRAZ ISLAND | AREA 12 ACRES
$1\frac{1}{2}$ MILES TO TRANSPORT DOCK
ONLY GOVERNMENT BOATS PERMITTED
OTHERS MUST KEEP OFF 200 YARDS
NO ONE ALLOWED ASHORE
WITHOUT A PASS

About the Author

Stephen Person has written many children's books about history, science, and the environment. He lives with his family in Brooklyn, New York.